THE
AZTECS

Peter Hicks

Thomson Learning • New York

Look into the Past

First published in the
United States in 1993 by
Thomson Learning
115 Fifth Avenue
New York, NY 10003

First published in 1993 by
Wayland (Publishers) Ltd
61 Western Road, Hove
East Sussex, BN3 1JD, England

Cataloging-in-Publication Data Applied For.

ISBN: 1-56847-058-4

Printed in Italy.

Picture acknowledgments

The publishers wish to thank the following for providing the photographs for this book: The Ancient Art and Architecture Collection 16, 18, 26; Biblioteca Laurenziana, Florence 7 (left), 19 (both); Bodleian Library, Oxford 8 (both), 9, 21, 28; reproduced by Courtesy of the Trustees of the British Museum 12 (top), 24 (top), 29 (both); Cephas Picture Library 5 (top, Nigel Blythe); E. T. Archive 15 (top); Werner Forman Archive *cover* (top), 5 (bottom, Biblioteca Universitaria, Bologna). 6 (British Museum), 7 (right, St. Louis Art Museum,), 11, 12 (bottom, Museum fur Volkerkunde, Berlin), 13 (Museum fur Volkerkunde, Berlin), 14 (University Museum of Anthropology, Jallapa). 15 (bottom, National Museum of Natural History, Smithsonian Institution, Washington, D.C.), 17 (both, British Museum), 20, 22 (top left and right, Museo Nazionale Prehistorico Etnografico Luigi Pigoroni, Rome), 23 (Museo Nazionale Prehistorico Etnografico Luigi Pigoroni, Rome) 24-5 (bottom, British Museum), 25 (top left, British Museum, top right, National Museum of Anthropology, Mexico City), Michael Holford *cover* (middle right, British Museum).

CONTENTS

Words that apear in **bold italic** in the text are explained in the glossary on page 30.

WHO WERE THE AZTECS?

The first people to enter the Americas came from Asia around 30,000 years ago. They were tribes of hunters and gatherers in those days, meaning they lived by hunting wild animals and gathering roots and berries. They were often on the move, following herds of animals and looking for new sources of plants.

By the time they had reached Central America many tribes had become farmers — they grew their own crops. This meant people did not have to keep moving and could stay in one place.

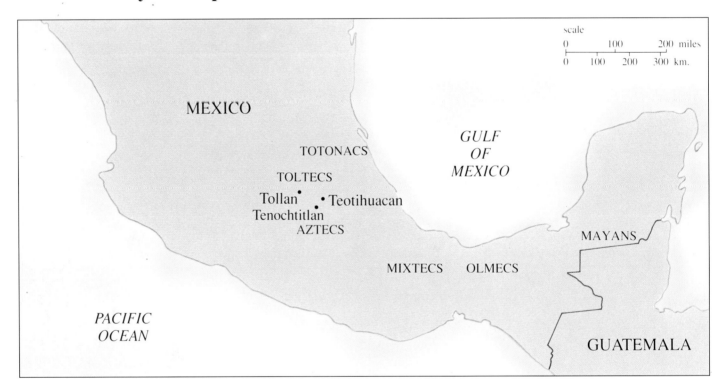

Many groups of people moved into Mexico, which in *ancient* times was known as "Anahuac," meaning the land between the waters. By A.D. 1200 one of these groups had developed into a separate tribe called the Tenochas, whom we know as the Aztecs.

However, all the best land had already been taken by other, stronger tribes, so the Aztecs had to wander for a long period of time searching for a suitable place to settle. All the other tribes of

Mexico at the time viewed the Aztecs with great suspicion. They often attacked and pushed the Aztecs out of land they tried to claim for settlements.

Finally the Aztecs moved to a number of small islands in the middle of Lake Texcoco, where by 1325 they started building a fine city called Tenochtitlan. The surrounding countryside was linked to the city by a number of *causeways* across the lake.

As you will see, Tenochtitlan was full of magnificent buildings, such as palaces and temples. This temple has survived in another part of Mexico, but the main temple of Tenochtitlan probably looked very similar. Study it carefully. Building it would have required great *engineering* skills.

Tenochtitlan — meaning "place of the Tenochas" or the place of the prickly pear cactus — became the base of a great *empire* that would last 200 years. It was an empire of great invention and beauty, but also of customs and beliefs that we might think cruel.

The story of the ▶ Aztec empire is an exciting one. As we trace its history, we will see a lot of objects from that time — what *archaeologists* call *artifacts.* Artifacts help us to find out how the Aztecs lived.

One reason that we know so much about the Aztecs is because they drew wonderful books called Codices. The Aztecs did not write with words, but used pictures instead. This is a page from the Codex Cospi, showing the gods of the sun and darkness. The beautiful colors in these pictures come from dyes made from vegetables and flowers.

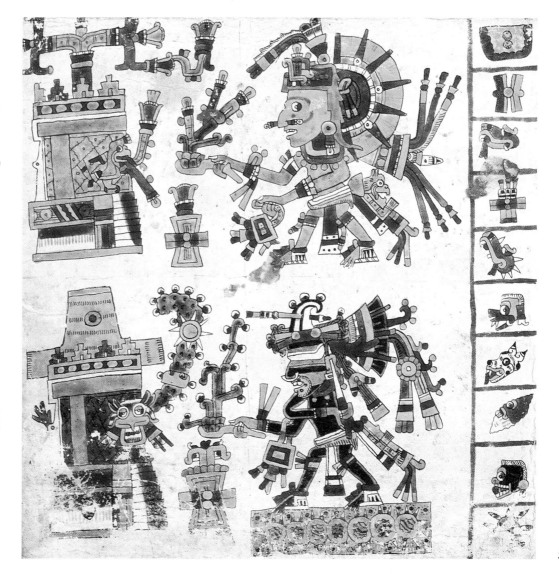

WORK AND FAMILY

Central to Aztec life was agriculture. We know that Tenochtitlan was built on small islands in a lake, so space for farming was limited. To overcome this problem the Aztecs built what have been called the floating gardens, or *chinampas*. These were woven reed baskets large enough to hold trees, filled with earth and fastened in shallow water. There were thousands of chinampas around the city and they provided vital areas of land for producing food. Mud was brought up from the bottom of the lake and used as fertilizer.

Families **bartered** goods that they needed—such as grass mats, pottery, and canoes—in a market. Throughout history all farming *civilizations* have used vast amounts of pottery. It was used for storage, cooking, and eating. Pots like these were often made from clay and decorated by women in the home.

◀ Maize—what we call corn on the cob— is being grown here. Maize was made into the main Aztec food: *tortillas*. These were flat, baked corn cakes, eaten by all families every day. The picture shows planting, **hoeing,** and harvesting a maize field, which was called a **milpa**. Aztec farmers helped each other in the fields. The land was not owned by one person but by groups of families called clans. As we shall see, war was very important to the Aztecs, and if a farmer was away fighting, his fields were looked after by others of his clan.

This statue seems to ▶ show a worker in the fields. He is carrying maize cobs and the heavy basket is attached to his head. But actually, this is a statue of a very important god, Quetzalcoatl, who will be discussed later. As "God of Life," Quetzalcoatl helped crops grow, which explains the five maize cobs on his back.

The family was a very important unit in Aztec life, but it had clear duties to the clan. Aztec men married at about the age of 20, women at 16. This picture is of a newly married couple. They have tied their cloaks together as a sign of their marriage. "Tied together" was an expression in Aztec society for marriage. When married they could live in either the man's clan or the woman's. Unlike other parts of the world at that time, Aztec women did have certain rights. A woman could own property, obtain a divorce if she was badly treated, and go to a court to plead for justice. Once divorced she could marry again, although if widowed, she had to remarry inside her clan.

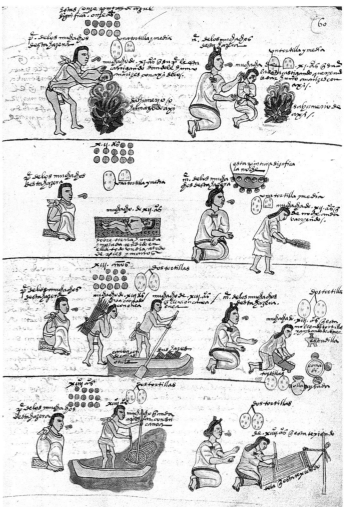

This picture shows the punishments given to naughty children. Also it tells us what skills older children learned. The blue dots tell us their age. The first pair of pictures shows children being held over a smoking fire for their wrong doing— a very unusual punishment by our standards . The next pair shows a boy being forced to lie out on damp grass and a girl having to sweep up. In the bottom four pictures you can see more children being trained in other skills, such as gathering wood, canoeing, cooking, fishing, and weaving.

THE GREAT CITY

Look at the ▶ splendid title page from the Codex Cospi. It shows how the city of Tenochtitlan was founded. The bird perched on the cactus branch in the center is an eagle. This comes from a very old and important Aztec legend. One of the gods told the wandering tribe to search for a swamp where they would find an eagle on a cactus with a snake in its claw. This was to be the site where the Aztecs were to build their city, Tenochtitlan.

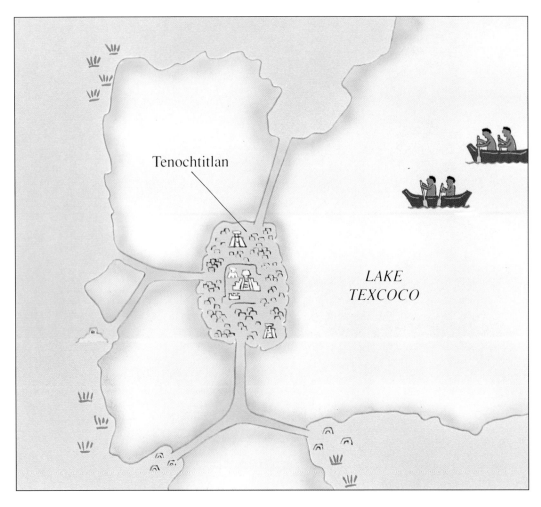

A visitor to Tenochtitlan would immediately notice the causeways (there were four of them) serving the city. Cleverly built, they were a system of drawbridges that could be lifted in the case of attack. At least two causeways carried an **aqueduct** that supplied the city with fresh water. As soon as the water reached the city square, it was sent through pipes to other areas or collected by people with jugs and carriers.

Many people lived ▶ in the city. Sadly, none of their homes exists today, but archaeologists have discovered what they may have looked like. Poorer people's houses were probably made by weaving tree branches and twigs together to form walls, which were smeared with mud and animal dung. The roofs were thatched.

The central point of the city was the great temple
of Huitzilopochtli, the sun god. It no longer
exists, but this is a temple that has been rebuilt to
show what an Aztec temple looked like. It looks
like an Egyptian pyramid. Placed at the top of this
stepped structure was the god house, containing
statues and images of the gods.

GODS

Aztec gods demanded human *sacrifices*. The only way to provide a constant supply of sacrificial victims was to go to war. It seemed as if the gods demanded permanent war. Aztec priests taught the people that Huitzilopochtli, the most important god, was a powerful warrior who fought with the moon and the stars to win each new day. If he was not fed human sacrifices for strength, he would be defeated and the world would end.

▲ Look at this beautiful but fearsome knife. The blade is razor-sharp flint and the handle is *turquoise mosaic*. Priests used this type of knife to perform human sacrifices at the very top of the temple, next to the god house. Huitzilopochtli, whose name means "hummingbird wizard," needed these sacrifices so he could triumph over the god of darkness.

What took place next can be seen here. ▶ The snakes falling from the victim's head represent the blood being spilled. The head was then stored in the temple.

The priests who carried out these sacrifices were strange-looking men. Their bodies were painted black all over and they had long hair, which was never washed or cut.

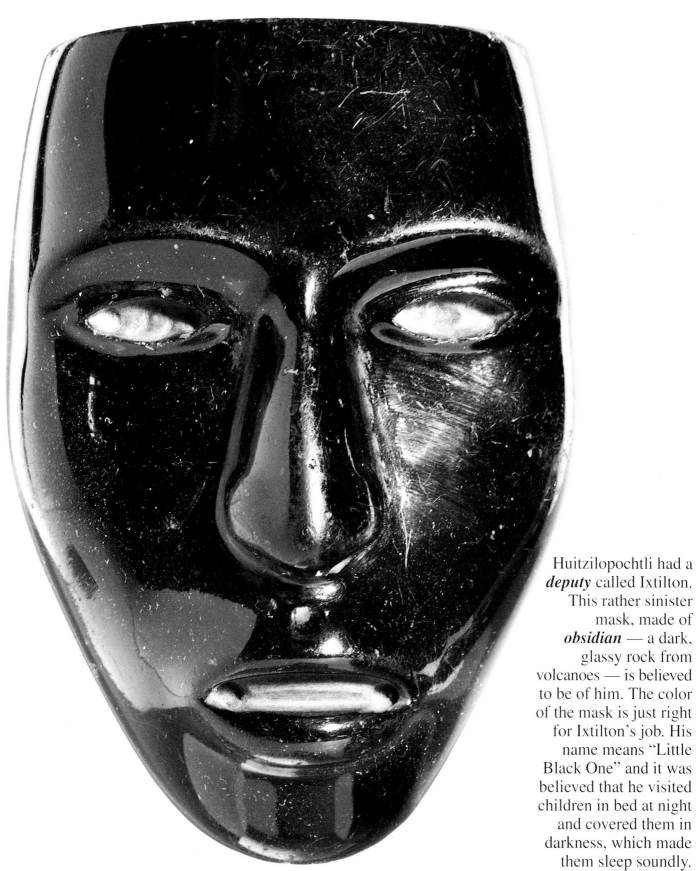

Huitzilopochtli had a *deputy* called Ixtilton. This rather sinister mask, made of *obsidian* — a dark, glassy rock from volcanoes — is believed to be of him. The color of the mask is just right for Ixtilton's job. His name means "Little Black One" and it was believed that he visited children in bed at night and covered them in darkness, which made them sleep soundly.

Another major ▶
Aztec god was
Quetzalcoatl. In this
carving he is wearing
his cone-shaped hat, a
necklace, earrings, and
a jewel in the shape of
a star on his chest. This
jewel stands for the
wind, showing that
Quetzalcoatl was the
god of the wind. An
object, probably a
piece of jewelry, has
pierced his nose.

Time was very ► important to the Aztecs. One of their calendars was divided into eighteen months of twenty days. This picture is an engraving of a great calendar stone, made 200 years after the Aztec Empire, showing how the Aztecs measured time. It has the twenty day names on it and the sun at the center. The real calendar stone would have been carved, and it would have been more than 13 feet wide. Time passed in a 52-year cycle. The years were counted by placing sticks or rods in a bundle, one for each year. When 52 had been collected, a new cycle began.

◄ An important ceremony called the tying up of the years was held at the end of each cycle. A bundle of rods, tied up with a rope, was placed on a fire and burned. The *symbol* of the final year covered the rods, as you can see in the middle of this carving. **15**

GAMES AND MUSIC

Aztec people loved to watch and play games. One of the most popular was "hachtli," a cross between volleyball, basketball, and soccer. It was a very fierce and rough game. Players could not use their hands, but they were allowed to crash into each other. The game was played in an I-shaped court, with walls about 8 feet high. The object was to get a rubber ball through a ring. This could only be done using elbows, legs, and hips. The players may have worn some kind of padding on these parts of the body.

◀ This is one of the stone rings used as a goal in hachtli. The ring was placed vertically on the wall instead of horizontally, and the team that managed to get the ball through the ring was the winner.

Music was important to the Aztecs. The beautifully carved instrument (above) is a drum. It was beaten on the two flaps at the top. You may have noticed that one flap is longer than the other. It gave a different sound when it was hit. The carved case shows a battle scene. Experts who have studied Aztec music believe it was very ***rhythmic*** and closely connected with dance.

The other two instruments (below) are flageolets, or small flutes. Music must have accompanied many ceremonies and festivals in Aztec life.

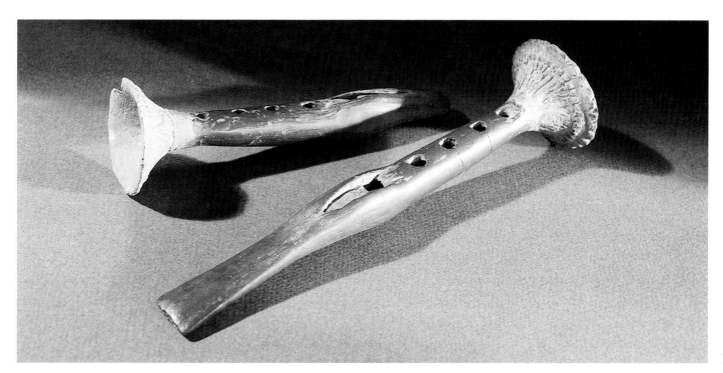

KNIGHTS AND WARRIORS

War was very important to the Aztecs. The gods demanded sacrifices, so prisoners of war had to be taken. When the Aztecs fought a battle they tried to frighten their enemy with drums and trumpets. They bombarded them with arrows and spears. The warriors then closed in and attacked with clubs. This usually made the enemy flee. When the opposing leader was captured, the battle would end immediately. The Aztecs soon built up a huge empire because of their successful wars.

This man is wearing and elaborate costume, which makes him look fierce. In fact, he was a very important warrior, one of the Eagle Knights. The best Aztec warriors were divided into two groups, the Eagle and Jaguar Knights.

18

The Jaguar Knight in this group was a scout who had to go out and look for the enemy and then report back with information about him. The Eagle Knight is shown in this group as well. To become a warrior was a great honor in Aztec society. At fifteen, young boys were taught how to fight and use all the different weapons. Each young *recruit* followed an experienced warrior into battle to learn the art of warfare.

Although these weapons look like thick ▶ swords, they are in fact wooden clubs which were made deadly by sharp obsidian flakes wedged in their sides. To defend themselves in battle the warriors used round wooden shields covered with animal skin.

19

This decorated shield is a back shield from the Toltecs, one of the tribes who lived in Mexico before the Aztecs. Aztec shields were very similar. Warriors wore them to protect their backs when they were fighting hand-to-hand.

Aztec warriors also carried one or two wooden throwing spears. Like the clubs, these spears, held by the warriors at the top and bottom of this picture, were made more dangerous by sharp obsidian blades added on to the sides.

Spears were much more deadly when launched from spear throwers, called *atlatls*. The spear was slotted into a groove in the back of the atlatl on the right and then held by a two-fingered grip. In battle, when the atlatl was hurled, it made the arm of the thrower seem longer. It also improved the warrior's aim and let the spear travel at greater speed. Other weapons used by warriors included bows and arrows.

▼ The burning of the enemy temple was a sign of an Aztec victory. In this detail from the Codex Cospi, the defeated warriors and the destruction of the temples can be seen in the background. Any prisoners who were not sacrificed were usually sold as slaves.

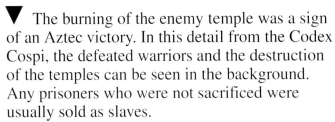

colhuacan. pueblo.

tenayucan. pueblo/

APPEARANCE

We have learned a lot concerning the Aztec way of life, and even about the way the people looked. Not surprisingly, most people took a great deal of trouble over their appearance.

Young, single women wore their hair long and straight. This mask shows a fashion popular with married women. On the mask's forehead can be seen the plaited hair curling around to the back of the head, where it stands up. Colorful ribbons were also woven into the hair.

Most women ▶ wore wraparound skirts, fastened by a belt. These skirts were fringed with ornaments to cover the knees. On top of the skirt a woman wore a colorful *poncho,* fringed with tassels and split at the center for her head. This statue of Lady Precious Green, a very important *fertility* goddess, shows some of these fashions. Notice her headdress and earrings and the tassels attached to her poncho.

▲ All the men wore *loincloths,* often with *embroidered* flaps at the front and back. Over these they wore decorated cloaks or capes, which were held in place by a knot over the shoulder. Everyone wore sandals with straps usually made of jaguar skin.

When attending ▶ special ceremonies, women would paint their faces. Look at these small objects. The designs on the two on the right are pottery stamps that were painted with bright colors and then pressed on the face. Women must have looked very striking when different colors were used.

The Aztec people wore spectacular nose pendants. The center of the nose was pierced so the pendant could be worn. These were more popular with men, but some women also wore them. The nose pendant shown here is solid gold, with the face of a bearded god wearing a very fine headdress. The detail is very impressive, showing craftsmanship of the highest quality.

Working with turquoise and shells requires great
care. These materials were used to decorate
masks, helmets, and shields. The base of this
helmet is wood, which has been carefully inlaid
with shells and turquoise. Because the helmet is
so delicate it would probably have been used only
on special occasions, rather than for protection.

MONTEZUMA AND THE GOD FROM THE EAST

At the top of Aztec society was the king. When he died his successor was chosen by the priests and army commanders. Members of the royal family, wise in the ways of religion and good in battle, were usually selected. The king had a huge palace and an army of people working for him. In 1502 a new king was chosen. He was Montezuma II and his name meant Courageous Lord.

This is the beautifully feathered headdress of Montezuma. He would have worn it when leading warriors into a battle.

Montezuma was a concerned leader. There was an Aztec legend that the god Quetzalcoatl would soon return to earth. On the very day in the very year that his return had been predicted, the Spaniard Hernando Cortés landed on the coast of Mexico, east of Tenochtitlan, with his *conquistadors.* The Aztecs believed that Cortés was in fact Quetzalcoatl and welcomed him as the returning god. Montezuma gave him many gifts, including this beautiful turquoise serpent. This drawing by a Spanish artist shows Cortés being welcomed in Tenochtitlan. Cortés is seated on the right. The woman behind him was very important. She is Dona Marina, a non-Aztec Mexican who came from the area where the Spaniards landed. She learned Spanish quickly and became Cortés' translator, making conversations possible between Cortés and Montezuma.

▲ Montezuma's palace was in the heart of Tenochtitlan. It contained many rooms; if you study it carefully you will find Montezuma. His personal bodyguards of 200 *chieftains* stayed in the room next to his.

Tenochtitlan.

Cortés, who could not believe his good fortune, cleverly managed to rule the Aztecs through Montezuma. The Aztecs thought that Montezuma was betraying them, and he was killed. Cortés then attacked the city, and in August 1521 claimed Mexico for Spain. After 200 years the mighty Aztec empire lay in ruins.

29

GLOSSARY

Ancient Belonging to a time long ago.

Aqueduct A tube or channel for carrying water.

Archaeologists People who study objects and remains from ancient times.

Artifacts Objects, such as tools or pots, that archaeologists study to find out how people used to live.

Atlatl A tool used by Aztecs for throwing spears.

Bartered Exchanged goods for other goods rather than buying them with money.

Causeways Raised roads or pathways across water.

Chieftains Leaders of tribes or clans.

Chinampas Floating gardens.

Civilizations Particular groups of people and how they live.

Conquistadors Spanish conquerors who claimed areas of South America for Spain 400 years ago.

Deputy Someone who stands in for a leader.

Embroidered Decorated with attractive stitching.

Empire A group of states ruled by one powerful state.

Engineering The design and construction of buildings, machines, roads, and bridges.

Fertility The ability for people to have children and for land to produce crops.

Fertilizer Anything that helps make plants grow in soil.

Hoeing Clearing weeds from between crops with a long-handled tool with a blade at the end.

Loincloths Pieces of cloth worn around the hips.

Milpa A maize — or corn—field.

Mosaic A design made up of small pieces of stone or colored glass.

Obsidian A dark, glassy rock from volcanoes.

Poncho A square cloak made of cloth with a central hole for the head.

Recruit Someone who is a new member of an army or organization.

Rhythmic Music with a strong beat.

Sacrifices Killing people (or animals) to offer to a god or goddess.

Symbol Something that represents or stands for something else.

Tortillas Flat baked corn cakes.

Turquoise A greenish-blue stone, used in jewelry and decoration.

Important Dates

30,000? B.C. First group of migrants reach the Americas
800? B.C. Olmec civilization established in Mexico
A.D. 100? Toltec civilization established
510 Toltecs build sun and moon temples at Teotihuacan
1168 Aztec tribes migrate into the Anahuac valley
1250 Aztecs live close to Lake Texcoco

1325? Aztecs occupy two islands in the middle of Lake Texcoco. Tenochtitlan — "place of the Tenocha"(prickly pear cactus) — is founded
1481 Construction of huge temple to Huitzilopochtli, the sun god, begins
1503 Montezuma II elected king
1519 Hernando Cortés arrives at Tenochtitlan
1521 Tenochtitlan captured and destroyed by Cortés and his conquistadors
1525 AZTEC EMPIRE IN RUINS

Pronunciation

Here are some of the Aztec words you may find difficult to pronounce:

HUITZILOPOCHTLI- *Weet-sil-o-pocht-lee*
MONTEZUMA - *Mont-eh-zoo-mah*
TENOCHTITLAN- *Ten-otch-teet-lan*
QUETZALCOATL- *Ket-sal-koat-l*

TEOTIHUACAN- *Tay -o-tee-wa-kan*
TEZCATLIPOCA - *Tess-kat-lee-pocka*
TEXCOCO- *Tess-koko*
TORTILLA - *Tor-tee-ya*

Books to Read

Bateman, Penny. *Aztecs and Incas, A.D. 1300-1532.* New York: Watts, 1988
Berdan, Frances F. *The Aztecs.* New York: Chelsea House, 1989
Crosher, Judith. *The Aztecs.* Needham Heights, MA: Silver, Burdett & Ginn, 1985
Hughes, Jill. *Aztecs,* Revised Edition. New York: Gloucester Press, 1986
Marrin, Albert. *Aztecs and Spaniards.* New York: Macmillan/Antheneum, 1986
McKissack, Patricia. *Aztec Indians.* Chicago: Childrens Press, 1985
Odijk, Pamela. The Aztecs. Englewood Cliffs, NJ: Silver Burdett Press, 1989
Shepherd, Donna Walsh. *The Aztecs.* New York: Watts, 1992
Unstead, R.J. *See Inside an Aztec Town.* New York: Warwick Press, 1980

INDEX